For Papa, with love.

—S. G. T.

For C and Z and a world full of magic.

—A. S.

Text © 2018 Sarah Grace Tuttle
Illustrations © 2018 Amy Schimler-Safford

Published in 2018 by Eerdmans Books for Young Readers,
an imprint of Wm. B. Eerdmans Publishing Co.
2140 Oak Industrial Dr. NE, Grand Rapids, Michigan 49505

www.eerdmans.com/youngreaders

Manufactured in China

27 26 25 24 23 22 21 20 19 18   1 2 3 4 5 6 7 8 9

ISBN 978-0-8028-5459-9

A catalog record of this book is available from the Library of Congress.

Illustrations created digitally

Hidden City

Poems of Urban Wildlife

Written by Sarah Grace Tuttle

Illustrated by Amy Schimler-Safford

Eerdmans Books for Young Readers

Grand Rapids, Michigan

NESTING

In the night
under the table
a mother mouse
scurries back and forth. She
rips paper
      carries
rips paper
      carries
rips paper
      carries
forgotten paper away
to build her nest.

WILD FLOWER

A dandelion
sinks its taproot
deep into the dirt,
spreads its toothed leaves,
and opens its yellow face
to the sun—
growing up wild
at the base
of a bus-stop bench.

MULTIPLY

Moss in sidewalk cracks
sends up delicate shoots
for shoes to
    tread on
    break off
    carry away
drop
where they grow into
new moss plants,
dense and soft
with delicate shoots
for shoes to tread on.

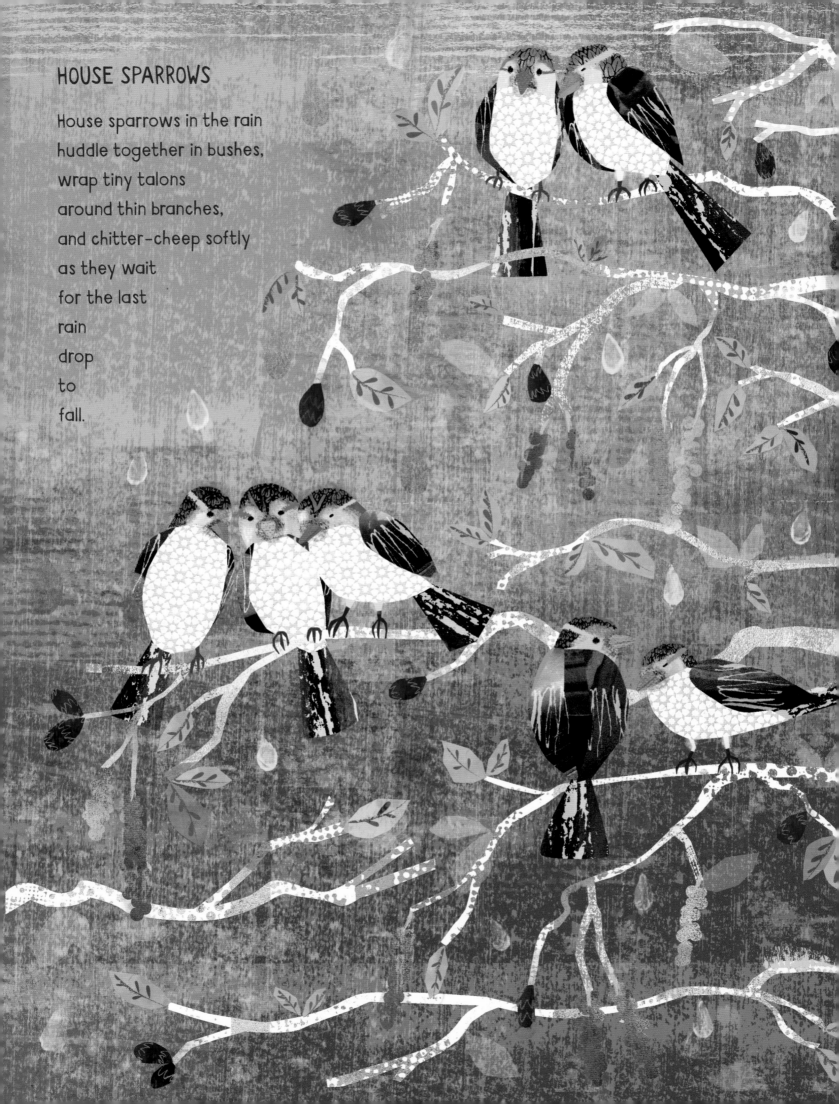

HOUSE SPARROWS

House sparrows in the rain
huddle together in bushes,
wrap tiny talons
around thin branches,
and chitter-cheep softly
as they wait
for the last
rain
drop
to
fall.

FAIRY RING

After a soaking rain
speck-sized mushrooms
swell with water
and expand
e x p a n d
E X P A N D
so quickly
that they appear
on the lawn
overnight.

COURTSHIP DANCE

In front of a fountain
    strut
    turn
    dip
male pigeons dance
    strut
    turn
    dip
parading rainbow feathers
    strut
    turn
    dip
to court a waiting female
    strut
    turn
    dip
who will choose for her mate
    strut
    turn
    dip
the one who dances best.

DEFENDING HOME

A red-winged blackbird whistles
Tweee!
Tweee!
and flashes his colors
before launching
from atop a cattail
into the sky
to chase a hawk
Away!
Away!
from the bit of marsh
beside the train tracks,
where blackbird chicks
hide in a nest
among the reeds.

HURRY UP AND WAIT

From a tall branch
a green inchworm
drops!
down on a silken thread,
dangles in the breeze
drops!
        dangles
drops!
        dangles
until its searching feet
touch earth,
and it digs.

Underground,
the inchworm
spins a cocoon
of dirt and silk
and waits
to become
a moth.

AT THE PARK

In the shade of a willow
two ducks dabble down—
heads underwater
tail feathers above
they sift through murky mud
and
      pop!
are upright, munching.

NIGHTTIME IN THE GARDEN

At night, snails
ooze from under
pots, rocks, porches, leaves,
logs, roots, bushes, walls.
They creep toward gardens
one by one,
munch through plants
one by one,
and return to their hideouts
one by one
before sunrise.

PAVEMENT FIGHT

A writing blob on the sidewalk
proves to be
ants
battling over
     where they can eat
     where they can mate
     where they can build.
Antennae wave
legs grip
mandibles rip
as two ant colonies
wage war.

FALCON FLEDGE

A peregrine falcon
six weeks old
teeters thirty-two stories above
busy sidewalks and a traffic jam.
She clutches the edge of her nest,
bobs her head,
and then
flap! flap-flap flaps her wings
leaps!
and fumble-flies down
to a roof across the street:
first flight.

COMMUNITY GARDEN

An empty lot has
grown over with
wild tangles of grass and aster,
bright dandelions,
wood sorrel, clover.
Now
bees and butterflies feast on nectar
ants build
snails crawl
and garden snakes sun themselves
by the graffitied wall.

SUNFLOWER BUFFET

Sunflower
pollen and seeds
can feed
   ant
   fly
   moth
   bee
   butterfly
   sparrow
   squirrel
   me.

ROOTED

Elm tree roots
spread out in a
shallow, tangled web.
Tough main roots and
soft tendrils
push through dirt
seeking
>   air
>   water
>   nutrients
all while clutching the earth
so the trunk
with its many branches and leaves
can stand tall.

ESCAPE

An exposed earthworm
dives headfirst
into dirt,
   muscles bunching
    body wriggling
it flees
underground,
where soil is moist
darkness is cool
and the earthworm
is safe.

BAT BREAKFAST

By a glowing street lamp
little brown bats
hunt
with a
        dart!
and a
        swoop!
and a hasty
        wing-scoop!
for moths
drawn by the light.

THE MOLT

In a corner by the cellar stairs
far from hungry birds
a harvestman
splits open its body
and pulls eight
l
o
n
g
l
e
g
s

from their old casings
until it can crawl away,
leaving behind only
an empty exoskeleton.

THE HUNTING LESSON

A mother raccoon
teaches her kits:
place paws firmly and
push
push again
push again
until
CRASH!
a feast spills out of the bin.
Bagels and fish heads and broccoli
all for the taking.

SKUNK SIGNS

Shallow holes and turned-up grass—
signs of
a skunk's nighttime hunt for
curling
crunchy
delicious
lawn grubs.

REST STOP

On scraggly grass
geese waddle about,
grazing in pairs
as they rest from flight.
Their tired honks
fill the silence
between
zooming cars.

CAMOUFLAGE

In the tree
behind the cemetery
a patch of
mottled light and shadow
half-hidden by leaves
is breathing.
As the sun sets,
it is waking.
Soon it will call
Hoo H-Hoo Hooo!
and launch into flight—
a great horned owl.

DINE AND DASH

A squirrel
    scampers
        to the feeder
gobbles
        up the seed
skitters
        down the street
scurries
        up the tree
to his warm nest of
brittle brown leaves.

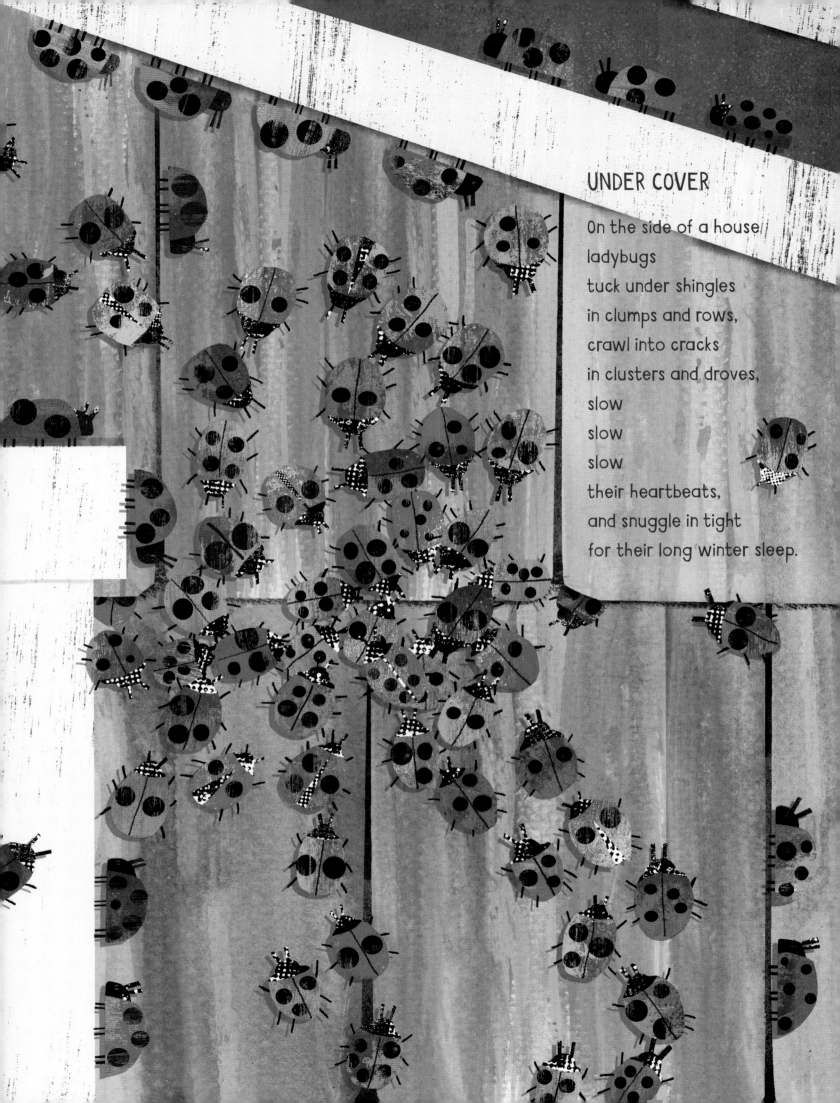

UNDER COVER

On the side of a house
ladybugs
tuck under shingles
in clumps and rows,
crawl into cracks
in clusters and droves,
slow
slow
slow
their heartbeats,
and snuggle in tight
for their long winter sleep.

REFUGE

Beneath
some old oak leaves,
a moth caterpillar
curls inside
a hollow acorn,
cozy in its winter home
as snowflakes
gather.

ONE IN THE BUSH

A feral cat
crouches under bare bushes
    neck stretched out
    muscles tense
    eyes fixed
watching
birds
peck at seeds in the snow.
One paw sneaks forward.
    Tail-twitch.
Ready . . .
    Dash!
    Claw!
    Bite!
A frenzy of feathers
and all the birds have flown
but one.
The cat
carries away dinner
to eat in private.

AFTER THE SNOW

Tracks trail
    two small footprints
    two **big** footprints
    two small footprints
    two **big** footprints
from under the porch
to a snow-laden bush
where a cottontail rabbit
nibbles bark.

WINTER SONG

A house cricket
crawls through a crack
and finds
a heating vent
where he sits to
chirp the song
that calls his mate.
Chreet . . . chreet!

FUN FACTS ABOUT THE WILDLIFE IN THESE POEMS

HOUSE MICE are noisy animals—we just can't hear them because many of the noises they make are too high-pitched for people to hear. Scientists even think that male house mice may sing to attract females, just like birds do.

DANDELIONS produce more flowers and make healthier seeds when there is more carbon dioxide (CO_2) in the air. So, as the amount of CO_2 in our air increases, causing climate change that threatens species all around the world, there may be more dandelions than ever.

SILVERY BRYUM MOSS grows well in sidewalk cracks because water running off the pavement gathers in the cracks and is held there. As a result, the moss still has plenty of water long after the rest of the sidewalk is dry.

HOUSE SPARROWS haven't always lived in North America. They were first brought here from Europe in the 1850s. Fans of the birds released them in cities across the country, and house sparrows are now found almost everywhere in the United States.

FAIRY RING MUSHROOMS grow mostly underground in white, thread-like bits. The underground part of a fairy ring mushroom grows in a circle, and the mushroom fruits (the part we see above ground) sprout up in a ring along the edge of it.

PIGEONS make milk to feed their young. Both male and female pigeons produce milk in their crop, an area in the neck that is used to store extra food. The parent pigeon must throw up the milk, and then drop it directly into the chick's mouth.

RED-WINGED BLACKBIRDS build their nests close to the water. To help keep their nests safe, male red-winged blackbirds act as lookouts, perching on top of cattails or nearby branches. They make a warning noise to alert other blackbirds to danger, and will even attack a predator, such as a hawk, if it gets too close to the nest.

INCHWORMS are experts at avoiding predators. Some inchworms drop from tall branches on a silk thread, dangling until danger passes. Other inchworms hide in plain sight by standing on their hind legs and looking like a twig or by sticking petals and leaves to themselves as camouflage.

MALLARD DUCKS have a spot near their tail where oil comes out. The duck spreads the oil over its feathers using its head and beak. The oil makes the feathers waterproof, so they can get wet without being damaged.

SNAILS survive in winter by hiding in a safe spot and sealing the opening of their shells with a layer of slime. When the weather warms up, the snails eat their way through the slime to get out.

PAVEMENT ANTS lay a trail of pheromones behind them when they walk. Pheromones are chemicals that ants and other animals use to communicate. This trail of pheromones is like a road leading other ants to food.

PEREGRINE FALCONS in the city nest on skyscrapers because these buildings are similar to cliffs—they have steep sides, with ledges and flat places to nest. Peregrine falcons also perch on skyscrapers to search for their favorite city prey . . . pigeons.

VOLUNTEER PLANTS like those that sprout in an empty lot are called "volunteer" because they grow without being planted by people. Many volunteer plants grow from seeds that blow through the air or are carried from place to place by animals. But some grow from seeds that have waited in the soil for years for just the right time. Seeds stored in the soil are called a soil seed bank.

SUNFLOWERS remove toxic metals and radiation from the soil. In 2011, after the nuclear disaster in Fukushima, Japan, people planted sunflowers to help the land heal.

ELM TREES are planted in city parks because they grow quickly and give excellent shade. Recently, these trees have been dying from Dutch elm disease. Thankfully, scientists have grown new types of American elm that are less likely to get sick, and now there is even a vaccine that can prevent elms from getting the disease at all.

EARTHWORMS breathe through their skin. People used to think that earthworms came to the surface when it rained to avoid drowning, but now we know that's not true—earthworms can breathe just fine in water. So why do they come out when it rains? That's still a mystery.

LITTLE BROWN BATS drink water by scooping it up in their mouths as they fly. If a bat gets knocked into the water by mistake while it is drinking, it will swim to shore.

HARVESTMEN may look like spiders, but they're not. Harvestmen can do all sorts of things spiders can't. For example, harvestmen breathe through holes in their legs called spiracles. And a harvestman can escape a predator by detaching a leg. The lost limb still twitches, distracting the predator so the harvestman can escape.

RACCOONS in the city get food from trash cans and other sources. Locked lids, bungee cords, and other barriers that humans create to keep wild animals out of our trash are all puzzles for raccoons to solve. The harder we make it for raccoons to get food, the smarter they become.

STRIPED SKUNKS aren't bothered by bee stings. A hungry skunk will even attack a beehive and can eat more than a hundred bees at once.

CANADA GEESE were once endangered. Thankfully, conservation efforts and the increase of lawn habitats in the last few decades have brought them back from the brink of extinction.

GREAT HORNED OWLS eat more kinds of prey than any other owl. Because of this, they can survive in many different habitats—including the city—so long as there are some tall trees for nesting and an open area for hunting.

EASTERN GREY SQUIRRELS bury acorns and other food in locations called caches. Squirrels can remember exactly where their caches are. A single squirrel might remember thousands of different caches.

LADYBUGS protect their wings with a hard casing called the elytra. The elytra is the part of the ladybug most people recognize—it is usually red, orange, or yellow with black spots. When a ladybug wants to fly, it opens the elytra and unfolds the long, delicate wings hidden beneath.

ACORN MOTHS lay their eggs in acorns that have cracks or holes in them. When it hatches, an acorn moth caterpillar will weatherproof its home by sealing all the openings with layers of silk that it creates, much like the silk a spider uses for its web.

FERAL CATS are the same species as pet cats, but they are wild animals that do not live with people. Instead, many feral cats live in groups, called colonies, that are made up of related female cats and their young. Feral cats in a colony will act much like lions in a pride—they live, eat, and raise their young together.

EASTERN COTTONTAIL RABBITS make two kinds of droppings—fecal pellets and cecotropes. Fecal pellets are like the poop people make—digested food made into waste. Cecotropes, on the other hand, are full of vitamins and nutrients. Rabbits eat their cecotropes every day!

HOUSE CRICKET males chirp to attract female crickets. The way a cricket chirps can give all sorts of information, such as the temperature outside, the size of the cricket, and even how good the cricket is at fighting off disease.

SUGGESTIONS FOR FURTHER INVESTIGATION

Bash, Barbara. *Urban Roosts: Where Birds Nest in the City*. New York: Little, Brown, 1992.

Downer, Ann. *Wild Animal Neighbors: Sharing Our Urban World*. Minneapolis: Twenty-First Century Books, 2013.

McCloskey, Kevin. *The Real Poop on Pigeons!* New York: TOON Books, 2016.

"Raccoon Nation," *Nature*, season 30, episode 7, directed by Susan K. Fleming, aired February 8, 2012 (Toronto, ON: PBS, 2012), DVD.

Read, Nicholas. *City Critters: Wildlife in the Urban Jungle*. Victoria, BC: Orca Book Publishers, 2012.